Contents

* easy

** medium

*** difficult

Words appearing in the text in bold, **like this**, are explained in the glossary.

The history of Christmas

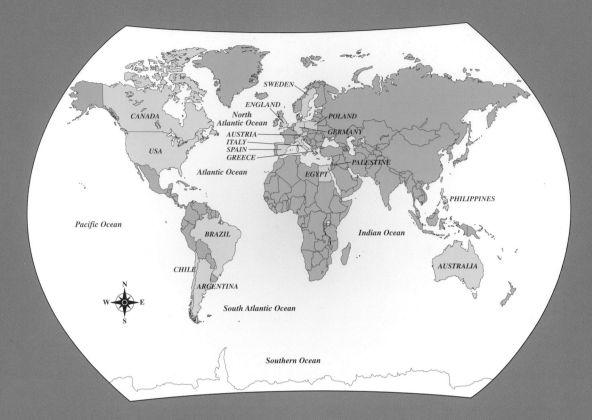

Christmas Day

On Christmas Day Christians celebrate the birth of Jesus Christ, the founder of Christianity. For most Christians, Christmas falls on 25 December, but in some places, such as Armenia, it is celebrated on 6 January. Christmas is one of the most important festivals of the Christian year and it is usually a time for parties and feasts, and often for giving presents.

The origins of Christmas

Although most historians believe that Jesus was born in spring, the founders of the early church chose midwinter as the time to celebrate his birth. They knew that people all over northern Europe already had a midwinter festival on 21 December, the longest night of the year, and they decided that midwinter would be the right time to celebrate the beginning of Christianity.

Many of our Christmas traditions have their roots in the ancient midwinter festival, when evergreens were used as decorations. In Scandinavia, people used to bring a huge log in from the forest and burn it as an offering to the Sun-god. This is the origin of the Yule log that people used to burn in their hearths at Christmas time.

What to eat at Christmas

All around the world there are different traditions about the food that people prepare for their big Christmas meal. Cakes and sweets are popular in many countries. In some places, such as Hungary and Belgium, these are wrapped in special paper and hung from the branches of the family Christmas tree.

Many German towns have Christmas markets like this one in Frankfurt.

In many countries the main Christmas meal is served on Christmas Eve. After the meal many people go to church, and this is where they will be at midnight, when Christmas Day begins.

The Christmas recipes that are in this book come from the countries shown in yellow on the map on page 4.

Ingredients

honey

glacé cherries

flaked almonds

cloves

mixed spice

ground almonds

candied peel

stock cube

cinnamon

nutmeg

Preserved fruit

Many Christmas recipes include cherries that have been preserved in sugar, and lemon and orange **peel** treated in the same way. You can buy **glacé cherries**, and other **candied** fruit, such as mixed peel, from supermarkets. The tradition of using preserved fruit began before people had fridges, when it was hard to find fresh food in the middle of winter.

Spices

Christmas foods often contain spices such as nutmeg, cinnamon, or cloves. Spices were very popular in the past because food was often eaten when it was rather old. The strong flavour of the spices disguised the taste of the food, even if it was going bad. Today we know that bad food is dangerous, but the tradition of using spices in many types of winter food has lived on.

Mixed spice

There are many different kinds of spices, as you can see if you look at the rack where they are on sale in the supermarket. Sometimes, instead of using little bits of several different spices, it is easier to use a ready-made mixture of ground spices, which is sold as 'mixed spice'. The mixture usually contains cinnamon, coriander, caraway, nutmeg, ginger and cloves. Note that mixed spice is not the same thing as allspice.

Honey

Honey can be dark and runny or stiff and light. A recipe will always tell you which sort you need. Some recipes might ask you to heat honey or sugar. It is important to have an adult with you when you do this because heated honey or sugar can become very hot indeed.

Stock

Cooks always used to make tasty stock by boiling up bones for hours and hours. The bones gave the water a rich flavour, and this stock could be used as a base for soups and stews. Today you can buy stock cubes and make instant stock by dissolving them in water. There are meat-, fish- or vegetable-flavoured stock cubes.

Nuts

Many Christmas recipes include nuts. Almonds are very popular, and they can be bought ready-chopped, toasted, flaked or ground. If you need to toast nuts yourself, take care as they burn very easily.

Some people are allergic to nuts. This means that it is very dangerous for them to eat food with even the tiniest trace of nuts in it. Always check that it is all right for your guests to eat nuts. Never serve food with nuts in it to anyone with a nut allergy.

Before you start

Kitchen rules

There are a few basic rules you should always follow when you are cooking.

- Ask an adult if you can use the kitchen.
- Some cooking processes, especially **frying**, and those using **boiling** water or syrup, can be dangerous. When you see this sign, always ask an adult to help you.
- Wipe down any work surfaces before you start cooking, and then wash your hands.
- Wear an apron to protect your clothes, and tie back long hair.
- Be very careful when using sharp knives.
- Never leave pan handles sticking out, because you might knock the pan over.
- Always wear oven gloves to lift things in and out of the oven.
- Wash fruit and vegetables before you use them.

How long will it take?

Some of the recipes in this book are very quick and easy to make, while others are more difficult and may take much longer. The strip across the top of the right-hand page of each recipe tells you how long it will take to make each dish. It also shows you how difficult the dish is to make: every recipe is either * (easy), ** (medium) or *** (quite difficult). Why not start with the easier recipes?

Quantities and measurements

You can see how many people each recipe will serve, or the quantities, by looking at the strip across the top of the right-hand page. You can multiply the quantities if you are cooking for more people. Avoid changing the quantities in a cake or a loaf, as this will alter the time that it takes to **bake**.

Ingredients in recipes can be measured in two different ways. Metric measurements use grams, litres and millilitres. Imperial measurements use ounces and fluid ounces. This book uses metric measurements. If you want to convert them into imperial measurements, use the chart on page 44.

In the recipes, you will see the following abbreviations:
tbsp = tablespoon   g = grams   cm = centimetres
tsp = teaspoon   ml = millilitres

Utensils

To cook the recipes in this book you will need these utensils (as well as essentials, such as spoons, plates and bowls):

- **baking parchment**
- baking sheet or tray, preferably non-stick
- bun tin or tray
- cake rack
- 20cm cake tin
- **chopping** board
- **fish slice** or spatula
- food processor or blender
- **grater**
- greaseproof paper
- heavy frying pan with a lid
- kitchen paper
- large non-stick saucepan
- measuring jug
- **ovenproof** dish
- pastry brush (for **glazing**)
- potato masher
- rolling pin and board
- scales
- set of pastry cutters
- sharp knife
- sieve or **colander**
- skewer
- **spatula**
- **whisk**

 Always take great care when using kitchen knives.

Shrimp snacks (Philippines)

The Philippines has a hot, tropical climate. The Christmas meal is usually a combination of light and tasty snacks. These prawn fritters are called *ukoy*.

What you need

90g shelled, cooked
    prawns
70g plain flour
1 tsp baking powder
pinch of salt
1 small garlic clove
1 spring onion
1 egg
pinch of white pepper
vegetable oil

What you do

1 **Chop** the prawns up into small pieces.

2 Mix the flour, **baking** powder and salt together in a bowl.

3 Crush the clove of garlic and chop the spring onion. Then **beat** the egg and mix it with the garlic and onion. **Season** with pepper.

4 Add 60ml of water to the egg and onion, then beat this mixture into the flour. It should form a thick, creamy **batter**. If not, add more water, a little at a time, until it forms a batter.

5 Add the prawns and mix them in well.

⊘ 6 Pour enough vegetable oil into a heavy **frying** pan to cover it to a depth of about ½cm. Turn the heat up under the pan until it is hot enough to make a drop of your batter sizzle. Take great care as the oil may spatter.

(!) **7** Drop a few spoonfuls of the batter into the pan. Cook for about 2 minutes and then, very carefully, turn the *ukoy* over with a **fish slice**. They should be brown on one side. Cook the other side for about 2 more minutes, until it is brown as well.

8 Take the *ukoy* out of the pan with the fish slice and drain them on kitchen paper. Keep them somewhere warm.

SEASONING WITH SOY

Try **sprinkling** a little soy sauce over the *ukoy*. Most people enjoy them even more this way.

Festive mushroom soup (Poland)

In Poland, the most important Christmas meal is eaten on Christmas Eve, before Midnight Mass, the special communion service that marks the beginning of Christmas Day. It is traditional not to eat meat at this meal; this simple, vegetarian soup forms one of several courses.

What you need

250g brown, flat-cap mushrooms
1 large onion
1 tbsp vegetable oil
2 vegetable stock cubes
juice of ½ lemon
150ml fresh soured cream
2 slices of white or brown bread
1 tbsp parsley, chopped

What you do

1 **Chop** the mushrooms and the onion.

(!) 2 Heat the oil in a pan and **fry** them for about 5 minutes, until the onion is **translucent** and the mushrooms are cooked.

(!) 3 Bring 1 litre of water to the **boil** in a saucepan and add the stock cubes. Stir until they have dissolved. They will dissolve better if you crumble them in your fingers as you are adding them to the water.

4 Add the lemon juice and the cooked onion and mushrooms to the vegetable stock.

5 Let the soup **simmer** for about 15 minutes.

6 Take the soup off the heat and add the soured cream, stirring very quickly.

7 Cut the crusts off the bread, toast it on both sides and then cut it into little squares.

8 Serve the soup in bowls, **sprinkling** a few squares of toast and some fresh, chopped parsley on top.

Chicken and meatball soup (Palestine)

Although most Palestinian people are Muslims, there are many Arab Christians living there too. This recipe is based on a soup that a Palestinian writer remembers her mother making on Christmas morning.

What you need

2 chicken stock cubes
½ onion
½ tsp grated nutmeg
1 tsp cinnamon
250g minced lamb
1 tbsp vegetable oil
50g long-grain rice
1 tbsp tomato purée
1 tbsp fresh parsley, chopped

What you do

(!) **1** Make the stock by **boiling** 1 litre of water in a pan and crumbling the stock cubes into it. Turn the heat off, and stir the stock cubes into the water until they have dissolved completely.

2 **Chop** the onion into very fine strips.

3 Mix the onions, spices and lamb together.

4 Using your hands, make the lamb mixture into small meatballs, each one a little bigger than a marble. Wash your hands.

(!) **5** Heat the oil in a pan, and **fry** the meatballs until they are cooked right through and nicely browned on the outside.

(!) **6** Reheat the stock until it is boiling, then turn down the heat so that it **simmers** gently. Add the rice, the tomato **purée** and the meatballs.

7 Let the soup simmer for about 30 minutes, until the rice is cooked all the way through.

8 Serve the soup in bowls with chopped parsley **sprinkled** over it.

Niños envueltos (Argentina)

The name of this recipe means 'babies in blankets', because that is what it is supposed to look like! It is a good reminder of what Christmas is all about – the birth of baby Jesus.

What you need

100g frozen leaf spinach
2 x 125g rump or sirloin
    steaks
salt and pepper
1 hard-boiled egg
150g cooked ham
1 tbsp butter
4 sprigs rosemary and
    some string
1 tbsp plain flour
1 tbsp vegetable oil
227g tin of chopped
    tomatoes

What you do

1 Allow the frozen spinach to **thaw**, and then **chop** it up roughly.

2 Put the spinach in a **colander** and, using a spoon, press it hard so that as much water as possible is squeezed out.

3 **Season** the meat with salt and pepper.

4 Chop up the hard-boiled egg and the ham into very small pieces.

5 Mix the spinach, butter, ham and egg together. Spoon the mixture on to the pieces of steak.

6 Roll up the pieces of steak. Tie them up and spear each of them with 2 sprigs of rosemary.

⚠️ 7 Sprinkle the flour on to a dish and roll the bundles of meat in it until they are entirely coated. Now heat the oil in a heavy pan and **fry** the pieces of meat for 1 or 2 minutes, turning them over at least once. When they are brown all over, add the tomatoes.

8 Put a lid on the pan, and cook it over a low heat for about 20 minutes. Check occasionally to see if it is getting too dry. If it is, add a little water to moisten.

9 Serve one 'baby' roll for each person, with potatoes and a green salad.

Savoury rice (Brazil)

This tasty rice recipe is popular on any special occasion in Brazil, including Christmas. Try it with turkey leftovers the day after Christmas, or cook it to go with another South American recipe – the Argentinian recipe for *niños envueltos* on pages 16–17.

What you need

1 small onion
½ chicken stock cube
½ tbsp olive oil
170g long-grain rice
2 tbsp **chopped**, tinned
    tomatoes
pinch of salt

What you do

1 **Slice** the onion thinly.

(!) 2 Crumble the stock cube into 350ml of water in a saucepan, and bring to the **boil**.

(!) 3 Warm the oil in a large saucepan, tipping the pan to coat the base evenly. Add the onion and **fry** it for 5 minutes, or until it is **translucent** but not yet brown.

4 Pour in the rice and stir for 3 minutes, until all the grains are coated with the oil. (Do not let the rice brown.)

(!) 5 Add the stock to the rice. Add the tomatoes and salt, and return the mixture to the boil, stirring it occasionally.

6 **Cover** the saucepan and turn the heat down low so that the rice is just **simmering**.

7 Cook for 20 minutes or until the rice has **absorbed** all the liquid in the pan.

8 If the rice seems to be drying out, add a little more water and stir well. If it seems to be cooked before 20 minutes, stop heating or it will turn mushy and sticky.

9 Pile the rice on to warm plates and serve immediately.

Jansson's temptation (Sweden)

In Scandinavia, winters are long, dark and cold. This warming potato dish is traditionally eaten around Christmas time. Anchovies are very small, salty fish that add real flavour to the dish. You can make the recipe without the anchovies, but then you will probably want to add salt along with the pepper.

What you need

500g **waxy potatoes**
1 onion
25g butter
8 anchovy fillets,
  chopped (optional)
black pepper
250ml whipping cream
1 tbsp chopped parsley

What you do

1 **Preheat** the oven to 160°C/325°F/gas mark 3.

2 **Peel** the potatoes and cut them and the onion into thin **slices**.

3 Rub some butter on the inside of an **ovenproof** dish. Use a round dish, no more than 20cm across. Set aside the remaining butter.

4 Place a layer of potatoes in the dish, followed by a layer of onions and a few anchovy fillets. Add another layer of potatoes, continuing until all the potatoes, onions and anchovies are used up. End with a layer of potatoes.

5 Grind a little black pepper over the potatoes. You will only need to add salt if you have not used anchovies. Now pour the cream over the potatoes.

6 Cut the rest of the butter up into small pieces, each about the size of a pea, and scatter these over the potatoes. Cover the dish with **greaseproof paper**.

7 **Bake** it for about 45 minutes. Remove the paper and turn the heat up to 180°C/350°F/gas mark 4 and bake for another 30 minutes, until the top is golden and the potatoes are cooked through.

8 **Sprinkle** with **chopped** parsley just before serving.

Mince pies (England)

Mince pies are served throughout the Christmas season in England. They are little pies filled with a fruit mixture called 'mincemeat'.

What you need

250g cooking apples
1 tbsp caster sugar
juice of 1 orange
300g dried, mixed fruit
150g shredded vegetarian
   suet or butter
150g brown sugar
30g mixed **candied** peel
30g **chopped** almonds
1 tsp mixed spice
1 tsp black treacle
2 tbsp plain flour
500g ready-made
   shortcrust pastry
a little milk
1 tsp icing sugar

What you do

1 **Peel** and core the apples, and then **grate** them.

2 Put the apples in a pan with 2 tbsp of water and all the ingredients, except for the flour, pastry, milk and icing sugar. **Simmer**, until the apples are soft.

3 Put the cooked mixture in a bowl. **Cover** the bowl and put it in the fridge. You can use it after 2 hours, but it tastes better after 3–4 days.

4 **Preheat** the oven to 200°C/400°F/gas mark 6.

5 **Grease** a bun tray. **Sprinkle** the flour on to a board, and then roll the pastry out as thin as possible. Cut 12 circles and line the holes in the greased bun tray.

6 Fill each case with mincemeat to the level of the edges of the pastry.

7 Gather up the remains of the pastry. Press it into a ball, then roll it out and cut lids from it, using a slightly smaller cutter. Dampen the edge of each lid with water before pressing it lightly over the filling.

8 Brush each mince pie with milk and then make a small slit in the lid with the point of a knife.

⊘ 9 **Bake** the mince pies for about 25 minutes, or until they are light golden brown. Sprinkle with sugar.

23

Ghryba shortbread (Egypt)

Christians in Egypt celebrate Christmas with many different kinds of cakes and pastries, including these shortbreads. Their Muslim neighbours use the same recipe to celebrate the end of their annual month of fasting, which is called Ramadan.

What you need

200g butter
60g icing sugar
200g plain flour
12–15 **peeled**, halved almonds or pine nuts

What you do

1 **Preheat** the oven to 180°C/350°F/gas mark 4.

2 Melt the butter gently in a medium, non-stick pan. Turn off the heat.

3 Add the icing sugar to the melted butter and mix in well.

4 Using a wooden spoon, add the flour a little at a time, stirring well. Keep adding flour until you have a soft **dough**.

5 By now your dough will be cool enough to handle. Roll it into balls of about the same size as a marble.

6 Flatten the balls of dough out to make small rounds. If the **baking** sheet is not non-stick, line it with **baking parchment**, and then put the rounds on the sheet.

7 Press an almond or pine nut into the centre of each dough round.

8 Bake the dough rounds for about 8 to 10 minutes, until the nuts are browned but the biscuits are still a pale cream colour. Do not let them go brown.

9 **Cool** the biscuits on a cake rack until they are hard and cool enough to eat.

Melomakarona (Greece)

The most important festival of the year in Greece is Easter, but this doesn't mean that Christmas goes by unnoticed. There are always plenty of good things to eat on Christmas Day – such as these little cakes soaked in honey.

What you need

125ml olive oil
25g granulated sugar
20ml freshly-squeezed
  orange juice
185ml runny honey
250g plain white flour
½ tsp mixed spice
½ tsp **grated** orange peel
1 tsp baking powder
100g granulated sugar
1 tbsp icing sugar
to decorate (optional)
  ¼ tsp ground cinnamon
  and chopped walnuts

What you do

1 **Preheat** the oven to 180°C/350°F/gas mark 4.

2 **Beat** together the oil, 25g sugar, orange juice and a third of the honey.

3 Mix the flour, spice, orange **peel** and baking powder together, and add it to the oil and sugar mixture.

4 Mix all these ingredients together in a bowl to form a soft **dough**.

5 Divide the dough into 4 pieces and roll them between your hands to make sausage shapes about 2cm wide. Cut each sausage shape into sections of about 5cm long.

(!) **6** Place the shapes on a **baking** sheet. If the sheet is not non-stick, line it with **baking parchment**. Bake for about 30 minutes.

(!) **7** Put the remaining honey in a small, non-stick pan, and add 100g granulated sugar. Heat gently until dissolved, and then let the mixture **boil** for about 5 minutes.

8 When you take the cakes out of the oven put them in a shallow dish. Pour the warm **syrup** over them. Leave them for 5 minutes.

9 Using a **fish slice**, put the cakes on a serving plate and **sprinkle** them with icing sugar mixed with ground cinnamon. You can also scatter over some walnuts if you like.

Stollen (Austria)

Stollen is a Christmas bread. It is meant to look like a baby wrapped in old-fashioned swaddling clothes, to remind people of Jesus as a baby.

What you need

grated peel and juice of a lemon
50g mixed candied peel
150g diced, mixed dried fruit
1 tsp nutmeg
200ml orange juice
500g white bread flour
100g granulated sugar
50ml warm milk
125g soft butter
7g quick-acting dried yeast
40g melted butter
100g marzipan
50g caster sugar
25g glacé cherries
25g flaked almonds

What you do

1 Put about ¾ of the **grated peel**, **candied** peel, fruit and nutmeg in a saucepan. Add enough orange juice to cover them. Add a little lemon juice.

2 **Simmer** these ingredients together for about 10 minutes, until the liquid is **absorbed**. Let the mixture **cool**.

3 To make the **dough**, mix the flour, sugar, milk, soft butter and **yeast** together with 120ml warm water. **Knead** for 10 minutes on a floured board.

4 Put the dough in a bowl and **cover** it with cling-film. Put it in a warm place to **rise**, until it has doubled in size. This will take about 30 minutes.

5 Put the dough back on the board and **punch it down** before kneading the cooled fruit into it.

6 Divide the dough in half, and roll it into 2 rectangles. Brush each one with melted butter.

7 Cut the marzipan in half and roll each piece into a sausage shape, the same width as the dough. Place a piece of marzipan on top of each piece of dough, then fold one side of each loaf over the other to enclose it. Press down on the tops of the loaves with a rolling pin to make sure that the dough is firmly stuck together.

⚠ 8 Let the loaves rise again for about 30 minutes. **Preheat** the oven to 190°C/375°F/gas mark 5. Then **bake** for about 35 minutes, until golden brown.

⚠ 9 While the stollen are baking, dissolve the caster sugar in 2 tbsp of **boiling** water to make a **glaze**. While they are still hot, paint the loaves with the glaze and **sprinkle** the **glacé cherries** and flaked almonds over them for decoration.

Amaretti (Italy)

These almond-flavoured biscuits are traditionally made in the south of Italy, where almonds are one of the most important crops.

What you need

200g ground almonds
100g caster sugar
2 eggs
1 tsp almond extract or
   2 drops almond essence

What you do

1 Mix the almonds and sugar together.

2 Separate the egg yolks from the whites. You can do this by breaking each egg, one at a time, into a bowl, and then using a spoon to carefully lift out the yolks.

3 **Whisk** the egg whites until they are stiff.

4 Mix the egg whites and the almond **extract** (or **essence**) together with the almond and sugar mixture.

5 Line a **baking** sheet with **baking parchment**.

6 Spoon the mixture on to the sheet, using only half a teaspoon of mixture for each biscuit.

7 Leave the biscuits at room temperature for 2 hours. In this time they will dry out a little, and this will make the finished biscuits crisper.

8 **Preheat** the oven to 180°C/350°F/gas mark 4.

9 Bake the *amaretti* for about 15 minutes, or until they are light golden in colour.

10 Allow the biscuits to **cool** thoroughly before serving.

PRETTY PRESENTS

Amaretti make a wonderful Christmas present. Wait until they are cool, and then wrap each biscuit up in pretty paper, before packing them into a decorated tin or box.

Christmas cookies (Canada)

There are lots of different recipes for cookies – almost every family in North America has its own 'traditional' one. Some people like to ice their biscuits with coloured icing, others use coloured sugar 'sprinkles' on them.

What you need

175g caster sugar
115g butter
1 egg
½ tsp vanilla extract or
   1 drop vanilla essence
150g plain flour
pinch of salt
¼ tsp baking powder
coloured sugar balls or
   other cake decorations

What you do

1 **Preheat** the oven to 180°C/350°F/gas mark 4.

2 **Beat** the sugar and butter together until they are light and fluffy.

3 Break the egg into the bowl with the butter and sugar, add the vanilla **extract** or **essence** and mix well.

4 Mix the flour, salt and **baking** powder together, and then add a few spoonfuls of flour mixture to the egg, sugar and butter mixture and stir well. Keep adding the flour and stirring until you have a soft **dough**.

5 Roll out the dough on a floured board until it is about 0.5cm thick and then cut out the cookie shapes. You could use a small biscuit cutter in the shape of a Christmas tree or a star.

(!) **6** Arrange the cookies on a baking sheet, leaving plenty of space between them as they will spread during cooking. Some decorations will need to be put in place before baking. Bake for about 8 minutes. Allow the cookies to cool slightly before you add the remaining decorations.

Christmas bread (Chile)

This bread is traditionally eaten on Christmas Eve, at a meal that brings the pre-Christmas fast to an end. It is very similar to Christmas breads and cakes that are eaten in Europe. This is because so many people from southern Europe settled in South America in the past.

What you need

110g butter
110g caster sugar
2 eggs
225g self-raising flour
110ml milk
1 tsp baking powder
100g **glacé cherries**
80g sultanas
30g **chopped** almonds
50g mixed **candied peel**
grated peel of 1 lemon

What you do

1 Preheat the oven to 150°C/300°F/gas mark 2.

2 Beat the butter and the sugar together with a wooden spoon until they are light and fluffy.

3 Break the eggs into the bowl one by one and mix well. Add the flour and mix gently.

4 Fold in the remaining ingredients and mix well.

5 Spoon into a round, **greased**, 20cm cake tin with a loose base.

(!) **6** **Bake** the bread in the oven for 1 hour 30 minutes. It is cooked when you can push a skewer, or knife, into its centre, and it comes out clean.

7 Allow the bread to **cool** for a couple of minutes and remove from the tin.

8 Cool completely and serve in slices. Christmas bread is especially tasty with butter spread over it.

Turrón (Spain)

Turrón is a special Christmas sweet from Spain. It is eaten at the end of a big family meal on Christmas Eve. The meal starts late – around 9 p.m. – and often includes seafood, meat and fish. The *turrón* is served last, with the coffee.

What you need

4 eggs
400g finely chopped, toasted almonds
200g pale, thick honey
200g granulated sugar
pinch of cinnamon
rice paper

What you do

1 Separate the egg yolks from the whites. You can do this by breaking each egg, one at a time, into a bowl, and then using a spoon to carefully lift out the yolks.

2 **Beat** the egg whites until they are stiff.

3 Mix in the almonds to make a **paste**.

4 Put the honey into a pan large enough to hold at least 2 litres and heat very gently until it is runny. Honey gets very hot, so be careful not to splash yourself.

5 Add the sugar and continue to heat until it has melted into the honey. Now allow the mixture to **boil** gently. Take great care, as boiling sugar is very hot indeed. Be sure to have an adult to help you.

6 Add the paste of nuts and eggs to the honey mixture and stir without stopping over a low heat for 10 minutes.

7 Line a large, shallow dish or **cover** a plastic chopping board with rice paper and pour the mixture on top. Use a non-stick **fish slice** or heatproof **spatula** to spread it out in a thin layer.

8 Allow the mixture to **cool**. **Sprinkle** it with cinnamon.

9 After about 12 hours, when the *turrón* has set, break it into small pieces and serve.

RICE PAPER

Rice paper is a kind of paper that you can eat. Used in many sweet recipes, it is made from plant fibre.

Candied sweet potato (USA)

Sweet potatoes are now grown in many parts of the world, but they originally came from South America. The best ones are pinky-orange inside, and look a bit like fat carrots, not potatoes at all. They are especially popular in the southern part of the United States.

What you need

5 sweet potatoes
55g margarine
115g brown sugar
3 tbsp orange juice
pinch ground
    cinnamon
275g white
    marshmallows

What you do

1 **Preheat** oven to 180°C/350°F/gas mark 4.

2 Wash the sweet potatoes and then cut them into thick slices.

3 Put the sweet potatoes into a large saucepan with enough water to cover them.

(!) 4 Bring the sweet potatoes to the **boil** and cook them until they are very **tender**. This should take about 15 minutes.

(!) 5 Remove the potatoes from the heat, and ask an adult to help you drain them, before you tip them into a large bowl.

6 Mash the sweet potatoes until they are smooth. Stir in the margarine, brown sugar, orange juice and cinnamon.

7 Spread the potato mixture evenly into a 20 x 30cm **baking** dish and **sprinkle** with marshmallows.

⊘ **8** Bake until the potatoes are heated through, and the marshmallows have puffed up and turned golden brown. This should take about 30 minutes.

Christmas pudding ice-cream (Australia)

Christmas comes in the middle of the Australian summer. Although some people have the traditional roast turkey, many others prefer a Christmas picnic, or a barbecue followed by ice-cream or fruit salad. This is an Australian recipe for a refreshing Christmas pudding ice-cream!

What you need

500ml vanilla or clotted cream ice-cream
50g ready-mixed dried fruit
½ grated eating apple
½ tsp each of cinnamon, nutmeg and ginger
1 tsp black treacle
4 **glacé cherries**, chopped
squeeze of lemon juice
100ml orange juice
to decorate, toasted hazelnuts

What you do

1 Keep the ice-cream in the freezer.

2 Put everything except the nuts and the ice-cream into a small, non-stick saucepan. The orange juice should just cover the fruit.

3 Bring the mixture gently to the **boil**, stirring all the time, and cook until the liquid is **absorbed** and the fruit is plump. This should take about 10 minutes.

4 Put the mixture into a small bowl, **cover** it with cling-film and put it in the fridge overnight.

5 Put a 1-litre pudding bowl in the freezer, also overnight. The next morning, take the ice-cream and the bowl out of the freezer; scoop the ice-cream out of its container and into the bowl.

6 Using a fork, quickly stir the fruit mixture into the ice-cream. You may have to wait a few minutes until the ice-cream is soft enough to mix, but do not let it become runny. You should still have lumps of ice-cream mixed with the fruit.

7 Serve the ice-cream at once, scooping it out into bowls and decorating with a topping of **chopped** nuts.

Spiced grape juice (Germany)

In Germany there are open-air markets at Christmas time, where all sorts of good things are sold for the festive season. A spicy, hot wine drink called *Glühwein* is sold to help keep out the cold. This alcohol-free version of the drink uses grape juice instead of wine.

What you need

1 **unwaxed** orange
1 tsp cloves
½ unwaxed lemon
1 litre carton
   unsweetened pure
   red grape juice
50ml runny honey
2 cinnamon sticks

What you do

1 Cut the orange in half, and then push the cloves into the skin of one half.

2 **Slice** the other half of the orange and the half lemon very thinly.

3 Pour the grape juice into the pan. It must either be a non-stick pan or one with an enamel lining. If you use an unlined metal pan it will spoil the taste of your spiced grape juice.

4 Add the orange with the cloves in it, and the orange and lemon slices.

5 Add the honey, using a non-metal spoon.

6 Drop in the cinnamon sticks.

(!) **7** Heat the pan until the juice has just begun to **boil**. **Simmer** for 20 minutes.

(!) **8** **Strain** the hot juice into a jug and serve in glasses or mugs. There should be enough for 4 servings.

WAXED FRUIT

Some oranges and lemons are coated in wax before they are sold. This makes them look shinier and more attractive. If you have to use waxed oranges and lemons in this recipe, you may find that some froth forms on top of the juice as you simmer it. Use a non-metal spoon to skim this off.

Further information

Here are some books and websites that will tell you about Christmas food and food for other festivals.

Books

A Christmas Companion, Recipes, Traditions and Customs from Around the World, Maria Robbins (Berkley Publishing Group, 1991).
Christmas Baking: Traditional Recipes Made Easy, C. Teubner (Barrons Educational Series, 1995).
The Feast of Christmas, Paul Levy (Kyle Cathie Limited, 1993).

Websites

http://www.geocities.com/HotSprings/Resort/8329/recipes
http://www.gti.net/mocolib1/kid/christmasfood
http://www.santas.net

Conversion chart

Ingredients for recipes can be measured in two different ways. Metric measurements use grams and millilitres. Imperial measurements use ounces and fluid ounces. This book uses metric measurements. The chart here shows you how to convert measurements from metric to imperial.

SOLIDS		LIQUIDS	
METRIC	IMPERIAL	METRIC	IMPERIAL
10g	¼ oz	30ml	1 fl oz
15g	½ oz	50ml	2 fl oz
25g	1 oz	75ml	2½ fl oz
50g	1¾ oz	100ml	3½ fl oz
75g	2¾ oz	125ml	4 fl oz
100g	3½ oz	150ml	5 fl oz
150g	5 oz	300ml	10 fl oz
250g	9 oz	600ml	20 fl oz
450g	1lb	900ml	30 fl oz

Healthy eating

This diagram shows you what foods you should eat to stay healthy. Most of your food should come from the bottom of the pyramid. Eat some of the foods from the middle every day. Only eat a little of the foods from the top.

Healthy eating at Christmas

A great deal of the food that we eat at Christmas is not very healthy! Many traditional Christmas recipes are packed with sweet and fatty foods. Enjoy your Christmas – but remember to leave room for foods that are better for you!

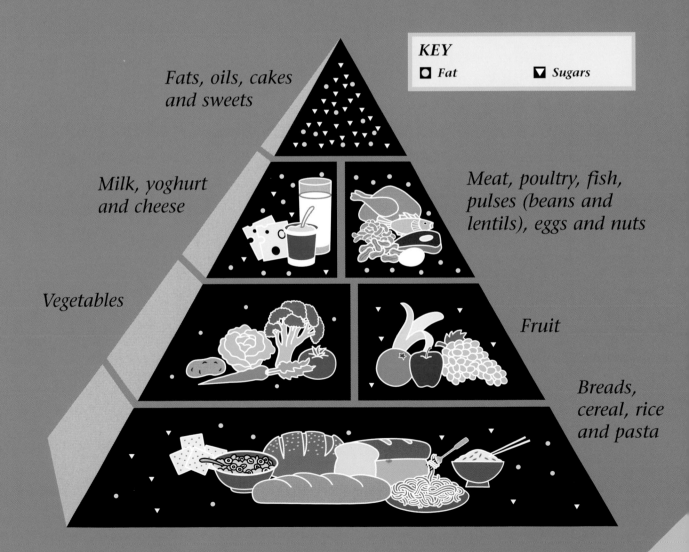

Fats, oils, cakes and sweets

KEY
☐ Fat   ▼ Sugars

Milk, yoghurt and cheese

Meat, poultry, fish, pulses (beans and lentils), eggs and nuts

Vegetables

Fruit

Breads, cereal, rice and pasta

Glossary

absorb soak up

bake cook something, such as cakes or pies, in the oven

baking parchment kind of non-stick paper you can use to line baking trays or cake tins, to stop things sticking to them

batter mixture of eggs, milk and flour used for coating fried foods, or making pancakes

beat mix something together strongly, using a fork, spoon or whisk

boil heat a liquid until it bubbles and steams

candied cooked in sugar. This is a way of making fruit keep for a long time.

chop cut something into pieces, using a knife

colander bowl-shaped container with holes in it, used for draining vegetables and straining

cool allow hot food to become cold. You should always allow food to cool before putting it in the fridge.

cover put a lid on a pan, or foil or cling-film over a dish

dough soft mixture of flour and liquid that sticks together and can be shaped or rolled out. It is not too wet to handle, but it is not dry either.

essence very strong flavouring, such as vanilla or almond essence. It is important not to confuse it with extract – you need only a small drop of essence, while you may need a teaspoonful of extract.

extract flavouring, such as vanilla or almond extract

fish slice utensil for lifting fish or other fried food out of a pan. It is like a flat spoon with slits in it.

fold in gently mix a light, airy mixture into a heavier one

fry cook something in oil in a pan

glacé cherries candied cherries, preserved in sugar. Other fruits can be treated this way, too.

glaze liquid, such as a mixture of milk and egg, used to make tops of bread or buns glossy during baking

grate cut into small pieces, using a grater

grease rub fat over a surface to stop food sticking

greaseproof paper kind of paper that does not absorb oil or fat

knead keep pressing and pushing dough with your hands so that it becomes very soft and stretchy

ovenproof will not crack in a hot oven

paste a thick mixture

peel remove the skin of a fruit or vegetable; or the skin itself

preheat turn the oven or grill on in advance, so that it is hot when you are ready to heat food

punch down kneading dough to get rid of big air bubbles. The air bubbles will be smaller when the dough rises for a second time.

purée mash, blend or liquidize food; or the blended food itself

rise grow bigger – dough rises when the yeast in it starts to work

season give extra flavour to food by adding salt or pepper

simmer boil gently

slice cut something into thin, flat pieces; or the piece of food itself

spatula blunt knife with a broad blade

sprinkle scatter small pieces or drops on to something

strain pour a liquid through a sieve. If a liquid has bits of fruit or flavouring in it, straining can get rid of them.

syrup thick, sweet liquid made from sugar and water

tender soft, but not squashy

thaw allow food that has been stored in the freezer to melt

translucent almost see-through. Onions become translucent when you fry them gently.

unwaxed not treated with wax to make it look shiny

waxy potatoes varieties (such as Estima and Maris Piper) with dense flesh that does not break up on cooking

whisk beat ingredients together to make them light and airy, or the utensil used for doing this

yeast substance used to make bread rise

Index